Francis Rother

Revelation of Genesis

Vol. 1

Francis Rother

Revelation of Genesis
Vol. 1

ISBN/EAN: 9783337310202

Printed in Europe, USA, Canada, Australia, Japan

Cover: Foto ©Lupo / pixelio.de

More available books at **www.hansebooks.com**

ፋግሬት ፡ ልኺኔ ፡፡

REVELATION OF GENESIS.

"THE LOST AGES."

FROM ETHIOPIAN MANUSCRIPTS OF AN ANONYMOUS,

IN EIGHT VOLUMES.

TRANSLATED FROM

AMHA' IC IN ENGLISH

BY

FR. ROTHER.

FIRST VOLUME.

———,

CAMBRIDGE :

THE HARVARD PRINTING COMPANY,

1890.

REVELATION OF GENESIS.

In the beginning God created the heaven and the earth. And the earth was waste and void ; and darkness was upon the face of the deep; and the spirit of God moved upon the waters.

The spirit of God is the beginning of all; thus it is written in the book of Moses; the Lord is the God of all spirits, and besides the matter of Moses spoken with God shall not be forgotten, as follows: Moses said unto God: Behold, when I come unto the children of Israel, and shall say unto them, The God of your fathers hath sent me unto you; and they shall say to me, What is his name? what shall I say unto them? And God said unto Moses, I AM THAT I AM; and he said, Thus shalt thou say unto the children of Israel, I AM hath sent me unto you; I AM was the beginning of all, and thus is the end of all.

After the beginning the waters were on the face of all deep, and also on the face of all high they moved. And the spirit of God moved upon the waters, and thus elements of fire came amidst the waters, but were scattering on all face of the deep and high. And there was light according to the word of God. And God saw the light that it was good, and God divided the light from the darkness. And God called the light Day and the darkness he called Night. And there was evening, and there was morning, one day.

In the beginning of creation there was evening, but when the light was amidst the waters thus there was morning and thereafter the light changed with the darkness, and evening with morning according to the wisdom of God. Because of the spirit of God the waters were stirring and thus produced the elements of fire. And the waters soared with the fires.

On the face of heaven there was no length and breadth, no height and depth before man's comprehension, and each of the elements of water and fire returned to its place according to God's word. And there was evening and there was morning, one day, and thus one day is one *Eternity*.

Because of the holiness of God the book Genesis was written by Moses's hand, and that did not omit nor add anything, but to the image of God to man it is given from child to child, to science, to study, to exploration, to the greatest work that ever comes before man, to the spiritual work.

On the Pentateuch in each chapter this word is written : God created in six days heaven and earth and the sea and all that is in them, and rested on the seventh day.

Before the face of God man was like the child whose intellect was hidden. And God being the true father put the man who was called Adam into a beautiful garden, and brought unto man the beasts of the field and the fowls of the air that he should see them and learn to give names to them. And also he gave to man wife. But when man from time to time received intellect he made sins pursuant to God's wisdom, for it was the will of God that man, the image of God, from child to child, shall augment intellect, and that from time to time knowledge and science shall multiply among men, and also that man shall learn to distinguish between good and evil. And God said to man from time of old, thus it is: Choose the good and abhor the evil, but God knew all this also, and in his heart said: The thought of man's heart is evil from his youth.

The darkness was in the beginning, but thereafter the light came, and thus the man was evil in his youth, but became good by his age. God made the firmament and divided the waters which were under the firmament from the waters which were above the firmament: and it was so. And God called the firmament Heaven. And there was evening, and there was morning, a second eternity. On the face of heaven a great many firmaments were created that are far mightier than the firmament of the earth, but God had not spoken on that creation that it was good ; and perhaps it may be that several firmaments will be annihilated at the coming time pursuant to God's thought.

And God said, Let the waters under the heaven be gathered together unto one place, and let the dry land appear ; and it was so. And God called the dry land Earth, and the gathering together of the waters called he Seas : and God saw that it was good.

And God said, Let the earth put forth grass, herb yielding seed, and tree bearing fruit after its kind, wherein is the seed thereof, upon the earth : and it was so. And the earth brought forth grass, herb yielding seed after its kind, and tree bear-ing fruit, wherein the seed is thereof, after its kind ; and God saw that it was good. And there was evening and there was morning, third eternity. And God said of

the earth, the dwelling of man, that it was
good, even of the third eternity creation,
but that God saw how the second eternity
creation was good it was not written in the
book of Moses.   Because of his holiness it
was so on the ground that man was not
able to explore the multitude of heaven
firmaments like the earth.   This reason
seemed stronger than that reason that from
the multitude of heaven firmaments several
will break in at the coming time.

And God said, Let there be lights in the
firmament of the heaven to divide the day
from the night; and let them be for signs,
and for seasons, and for days and years;
and let them be lights in the firmament of
‘heaven to give light upon the earth: and it
was so.   And God made the two great
lights; the greater light to rule the day,
and the smaller light to rule the night; he
made the stars also.   And God set them
in the firmament of the heaven to give
light upon the earth and to rule over the
day and over the night, and to divide the
light from the darkness: and God saw that

it was good. And there was evening, and there was morning, fourth eternity.

And God created the great sea monsters and every living creature that moved, which the waters brought forth abundantly after their kinds; and every winged fowl after its kind; and God saw that it was good. And God blessed them, saying, Be fruitful, and multiply, and fill the waters in the seas, and let fowl multiply on the earth. And there was evening, and there was morning, fifth eternity.

And God said, Let the earth bring forth the living creature after its kind, cattle and creeping thing, and beast of the earth after its kind: and it was so. And God made the beast of the earth after its kind, and the cattle after their kind, and everything that creeps upon the ground after its kind; and God saw that it was good. And God said, Let us make man in our image after our likeness; and let them have dominion over the fish of the sea, and over the fowl of the air, and over the cattle, and over all the earth, and over every creeping thing that creeps upon the earth.

And God created man in his own image, in the image of God created he him : male and female created he them. And God blessed them : and God said unto them, Be fruitful, and multiply and replenish the earth and subdue it, and have dominion over the fish of the sea, and over the fowl of the air, and over every living thing that moves upon the earth. And God said, Behold, I have given you every herb yielding seed, which is upon the face of all the earth, and every tree and every fruit of the tree yielding seed; to you it shall be for food; and to every beast of the earth, and to every fowl of the air, and to everything that creeps upon the earth, wherein there is living soul, I have given every green herb for food; and it was so. And God saw everything that he had made, and, behold, it was very good. And there was evening, and there was morning, sixth eternity.

And the heaven and the earth were fin-

ished; and all the host of them. And on
the seventh day God finished his work
which he had made, and he rested on the
seventh day from all his work which he
had made. And God blessed the seventh
day and hallowed it, because in it he rested
from all his work which God had created
and made.

God created the heaven and the earth
and all their host in six eternities, and
rested on the seventh eternity. And
when God created all them, there was a
great deal of pain and sorrow in the
spirit of God which man from generation
to generation shall never be able to comprehend thereof. And after God had
created man in his image, after his likeness, he rested on the seventh eternity, for
he saw how the creation of man was very
good.

The heaven, and the earth, and all their
host were created from the first eternity
until second eternity connectedly, and
thus from second eternity until third
eternity connectedly, and from third

eternity until fourth eternity connectedly, and from fourth eternity until fifth eternity connectedly, and from fifth eternity until sixth eternity connectedly, and on the seventh eternity God rested from all work that he had made. And God blessed the seventh eternity and hallowed it, for before God it was there written that the heaven and the earth and all the host of them were very good. The creation of man in God's image, after his likeness, is a perfect work of the Lord. And after God had given to man dominion over all beasts that are on the earth, and over all things that move in the seas, and over all things that soar in the air, then he rested unto the seventh eternity. Therefore God gave commandment to man. Thus said he:

Remember the Sabbath day to keep it holy. And thus it becomes very much to man from generation to generation that he learn to remember the seventh day and to hallow it. And God said unto man: This Sabbath be a sign unto you of the covenant that is established between me

and you. And in the book of Moses it
was written that the commandment in
behalf of the Sabbath shall be kept by the
children of Israel, and by the strangers
that dwell among them.

And God had driven out Adam from the
garden because of his disobedience, and
thus it shall not become to the children of
Israel that they transfer the Sabbath from
the seventh day to another day of the
week. And God brought forth manna of
two-fold unto the children of Israel on the
sixth day for the following day, for the
Sabbath, but from the people some men
went out on the seventh day to gather and
found none. And the Lord said unto
Moses: How long refuse ye to keep my
commandments and my laws? See, for
that the Lord hath given you the Sabbath;
therefore he giveth you on the sixth day
the bread of two days; abide ye every
man in his place, let no man go out of his
place on the seventh day. Because of the
holiness of God appeared the Lord before
the children of Israel in cloud and fire, and

said : Remember the Sabbath day to keep
it holy. Six days shalt thou labor and
do all thy work ; but the seventh day is a
Sabbath unto the Lord thy God ; in it thou
shalt not do any work, thou, nor thy son,
nor thy daughter, nor thy man servant,
nor thy maid-servant, nor thy cattle, nor
thy stranger that is within thy gates ; for
in six days the Lord made heaven and
earth, the sea, and all that in them is, and
rested the seventh day ; wherefore the
Lord blessed the Sabbath day and hallowed
it.

For these words God did not add more
things nor did he also omit anything. But
God had spoken that man, the image of
God, and his likeness shall be like the
creator, and by the time shall be perfect
from generation to generation.

And man by his heart shall ask himself :
What is the Sabbath of the Lord ? What
shall I do to hallow the Sabbath ? And
every man himself shall learn the reason
of the Sabbath, and when he understands
that in meeting and school he shall praise

his father, the creator, by offerings of righteousness, by wise talk, by good works. And when man understands the reason of the Sabbath out from his whole soul, the day of the Sabbath shall be unto man like the day of delight, like time of hallelujah.

And Christ said to his brethren, the Jews, the Sabbath is for man's sake, the man is not for Sabbath's sake, and thus the son of man is Lord of the Sabbath.

And when man understands the reason of the Sabbath fully he will hallow that day with joy, and thus man is Lord of the Sabbath. God, for his image's sake, for man's sake, had labored six eternities with a great deal of pain and sorrow, and after he created man perfectly he rested on the seventh eternity. Therefore God commanded that following after the fourth commandment to man, thus it is: Honor thy father and thy mother, that thy days may be long upon the land which the Lord thy God giveth thee. And man was created in the image of God. And after man had begotten his child with pain and

sorrow, this child himself shall know how
much it becomes for him to honor his
father and his mother, but when the child
does evil before his father the latter shall
be stricken with pain and sorrow, and thus
God shall be stricken with pain and sorrow when man does evil before his creator.
This history ought not to be forgotten, as
follows: And when men began to multiply
on the face of the earth, and daughters
were born unto them, the children of God
saw the daughters of men that they were
fair: and they took them wives of all that
they choose.   And the Lord said, My
spirit shall not strive with man forever,
for that he also is flesh ; yet shall his days
be a hundred and twenty years.   Monsters
of men were on the earth in those days,
and also after that, when the sons of God
came in unto the daughters of men, and
they bare children to them ; the same were
the mighty men which were of old, men
of renown.   And the Lord saw that the
wickedness of man was great in the earth,
and that every imagined thought of his

heart was only evil continually. And it repented the Lord that he had made man on the earth, and it grieved him at his heart. And the Lord said, I will destroy man whom I have created from the face of the ground; both man, and beast, and creeping thing, and fowl of the air; for it repents me that I have made them. But Noah found grace before the Lord, for Noah was a righteous man, was perfect amidst his generation, and walked with God. When God thought to annihilate man by the flood of waters it grieved him exceedingly at his heart, for man, the likeness of God, was created after six eternities with a great deal of pain and sorrow, for God expected from his son, the man, that he walk with God and be perfect after the spirit of his creator. And, behold, the earth was corrupt before God, and the earth was filled with violence. And God saw the earth, and, behold, it was corrupt; for all flesh had corrupted his way upon the earth. And God was in his heart exceedingly aggrieved, for on that

cause he was hindered to rest his Sabbath,
and for the men, the children of God had
perverted the way of their creator by
wickedness and violence, and had polluted
the Sabbath of the Lord foully.

Before the flood of waters after Adam
there were several wise men that preached
before their people the word of the Lord;
and out from them was Enoch, called in
the book of Moses. Many books were lost
by the flood of waters that were taught by
God to wise men, in order to teach other
men for good works.

Adam was brought up in the beautiful
garden, for he was like a little child
before the Lord. And when Adam prospered in body and spirit, his father, the
Lord, brought the beast of the field and
the fowl of the air unto him that he
should learn dominion over them. And
among these animals was the serpent,
called in the Pentateuch, thus it is: And
the serpent was more subtle than any
beast of the field which the Lord God had
made.

PREFACE.

The Bible is a common property of mankind, a sanctuary in every household.

But many say, the old reverend book is pretty well worn out because of breeding of modern intellect and thought among mankind.

And the other many mourn it, the decay of the religious tower. But all this is not the fault of the Lord, but of men, because they clothe the pillar of religion with rubbish of human convenience and with rust of narrow mind.

The anonymous Author, it seems to the translator, has stretched forth his hand to purify the old Bible from all the atmosphere that ought not to envelope it, to the injury of modern mankind at large; the " New Bible," or New Pentateuch, as the reader may choose to call it, sets forth to

proclaim the majesty of the living God.
It bears witness against all, and at the
same time divides favor unto all alike,
regardless of birth and race.

The Great Problems that are set up
ever before mankind are treated in the
" New Bible " as follows:

How was the creation by God in the
six days of the Lord?

What means the sabbath of God in the
seventh day of the Lord?

Who were the races that reigned there
before Adam?

Why were Adam and Eve called the
parents of present mankind?

How was woman created of man?

Was the sin of Adam a curse for mankind?

Who was the serpent who was there
with Adam?

What was the Great Sign of God unto
Cain that nobody shall punish him for his
fratricide?

Who were the children of God on earth
up to Noah's time, up to the flood?

What means the righteousness of Enoch?

Who was Noah, the builder of the Great Ark?

What natural causes led to the great flood of waters?

The first Ethiopian volume, as written by the anonymous Author, holds a short review about the known stories from the creation up to the building of Babel, and scatters here and there new passages and stories, but the other seven volumes dwell exclusively on the lost ages up to the time of Noah.

THE TRANSLATOR.

New York, 1890.

IS MAN GODLIKE?

Praise the Lord.
Look upon thy fort,
The great I AM liveth,
Put his name in song and harp,
Ring of all the good he giveth,
Call out into pagan ears, dull and sharp,
God's grace ascendeth over heaven
Up, down, to dust, unto human leaven
Hear the voice of the Lord,
The Creator openeth his mouth,
From star to star goeth the decree forth,
Man is Godlike in and out,
In God's image is he created,
Wonder ye, dust breatheth,
See ye, stone is clothed with flesh,
Be ye of the divine decree proud,
For he maketh thee of cement fresh,
Angels of truth cry out,

Man is but an endless something
Of the image of the great Laborer,
Humanity is only any infinite anything
Of the likeness of the Creator.
Voice of wonder here,
Voice of awe there,
Is dust like God:
In God's image is man good:
In human skull God's spirit stayeth:
Yea, the mouth of the Lord sayeth,
Nay, He decreeth in the angel's chorus.
Behold, He is become as one of us,
Man knoweth good and bad,
Even he, the crown of the Lord's Sabbath.

THE AUTHOR.

And the earth was created under the soaring fires of the third eternity, and brought forth the grass and the tree wherein is seed that grew from a little seed. But for the earth's sake, for herself's sake, two great lights were finnished to give light upon the earth, and signs for day, season, and years. And the stars were made after the spirit of God, but on the endless face of heaven a great many firmaments were created like the earth, and of them there is no end. And these firmaments were called stars like the earth. And unto the Lord from eternity to eternity there is no Sabbath because of the creation of new stars. But for this earth, after God had created man on the face thereof, unto the Lord there was Sabbath in the time of the seventh eternity. Therefore this reason will be very well understood how God did not say that the creation of heaven firmaments which he made in the second eternity was good, and how the book of Moses was silent on this matter.

From the midst of the fourth eternity
until the beginning of the fifth eternity
the seed of fish moved in the water, having living soul, and from this little seed
many fishes grew and multiplied, and at
the last time great sea monsters became
living inside of the water, and also from
the water the seed of fowl came; and
afterwards the fowl began to soar under
the heaven, and the creation of them was
by the warmth of the sun finished at the
end of the fifth eternity. From the midst
of the fifth eternity until the beginning
of the sixth eternity, because of the
warmth of the sun, the seed of worm came
from the water, and thereafter the creeping thing began to move upon the earth,
and from this creeping thing out the beast
of the field grew living after its kind, and
unto their completion grew pursuant to the
spirit of God.

In the midst of the sixth eternity, from
the monkey out, the seed of man began to
grow, and in a warm and good country
(garden) prospered unto its completion

pursuant to the spirit of God. And before Adam the likenesses of man were destroyed from the face of the earth pursuant to the spirit of God. And when Adam became living in the garden at the end of the sixth eternity, God saw that man, the likeness of God, of the image of his father, was good. And, blessing man, he gave to him dominion over the beast of the field. And God again saw the creation of six eternities, and, behold, all this was very good, and in the seventh eternity, sitting on the throne of heaven, he rested.

Therefore God said by the hand of the wise and prophets to the children of Israel that they shall remember to hallow the Sabbath of the Lord. And concerning the coming time of the earth God expected that through the hand of Israel man be perfect in his spirit pursuant to God's spirit. And the perfection of the spirit that is in man is a great, and hard, and quite painful work before the Lord, but men shall struggle one with another by a great deal of wickedness and trouble for several times, and among men intellect, and knowledge shall multiply, and henceforth the longing of God for man's perfection will be fulfilled at that time.

From the remains of animals and creeping things there were some living until the birth of Adam, having language of man, and thûs the serpent was playing before Adam and his wife in the garden like other animals which God had brought to them. Adam and his wife liked the serpent, for he was more subtle than other animals. The serpent and other animals that were in the garden were stricken with fear before Adam and his wife pursuant to God's spirit. Adam and his wife were themselves naked, but they learned dominion over these animals. And the parents of Adam, and also the parents of his wife, with those together, perished at a former time from the face of the earth, pursuant to the spirit of God, for they were not able to understand the rights and commandments of the Lord. And after the creeping thing had multiplied on the

earth under the sun, two sexes came in the
fifth eternity time which were called male
and female, and because of the holiness of
God thus a short word was written in the
Pentateuch concerning the creation of
Adam and his wife, that the generation of
Adam and Noah shall understand this
word by their child-like spirit and shall
learn the fear of their father, God.

From the rib of the male creeping thing
went forth the female creeping thing at
the time of sleeping in its lustfulness. And
on this account the word of the Pentateuch
will be understood concerning the creation
of Adam and his wife.

And when the creeping thing began to
move under the heat of the sun these took
by little and little to feeling, and thereafter smelling entered through its nostrils,
and these became living souls pursuant of
God's spirit. And the creeping things
without number were perishing at the
time of sunset, and thereof remained few
that could grow pursuant to God's spirit.
And these creeping things had a good

smelling, but these were blind, without eyes, and when these raised their nostrils unto the sun, these, by means of hard longing took to seeing ; and at that time fear went forth over these creeping things because of the hard struggle that was among them, and thus by little and little took to good hearing. And from these creeping things the fowl of the air, the beast of the field, and cattle all went forth after its kind from the fifth eternity until the sixth eternity.

And Adam was the first man who received the first right, and commandment by God, his father. But the serpent and other beasts from the lost generation having man's language, and likeness of man were playing near by of Adam and his wife in the garden, but the likeness of God had not yet come upon them ; and therefore they served to Adam and his wife with fear. And God brought some of these remaining animals into the garden to tempt man.

And Adam and his wife grew very

largely in their body, and also had very
much strength, and therefore all beasts
which were near by them feared Adam
and his wife.

But after Noah's time men began to
diminish in their bodies, and also their
lifetime became short pursuant to God's
spirit. And this case was so, for intellect
and knowledge multiplied among men that
they may have dominion over all animals
that are on the earth and in the sea.

The serpent ate from the fruit of the
tree, but not from dust of the earth; he
ate with his master Adam, and his wife
together in the garden, but Eve liked the
serpent much, and told to him the commandment of God. And the serpent having yet not the likeness of God had evil,
and subtle thoughts, and also ate before
Eve from the fruit of the tree which God
had commanded to man not to eat from.
And the knowledge of Adam to distinguish
between good and evil was still hidden, and
pursuant to God's wisdom, was opened by
the mouth of the serpent. Adam and his

wife were from their race the first, who became aware of their nakedness; they sewed fig-leaves together, and thus made themselves aprons. The friendship that was then between Eve and the serpent changed into bitter enmity pursuant to God's spirit. The likeness of the serpent is sin, for it is of the likeness of man, but not of God. And therefore it will be understood that the thought of God be perfectly high and sublime before the children of men. Thus said he:

Thou sin, I will put enmity between thee and man, between thy seed, and his seed; it shall bruise thy head, and thou shalt bruise his heel. And when God saw how Adam and his wife after the likeness of God knew good and evil and put aprons over their nakedness, thus said he: Behold, the man is become as one of us, to know good and evil, and now, lest he put forth his hand, and take also of the tree of life and eat, and live forever, therefore God the Lord sent him forth from the garden of Eden to till the earth whereon he was created. But according to the wisdom of God, the disobedience of Adam was going to good, and became a great blessing for the children of Adam. And it is the will of God the creator, that the children of Adam shall till the earth, and thus struggling with sorrow and need, shall walk until to the likeness of God, for he had created the earth and all that is in the earth in six eternities, with a great deal of pain and sorrow. And God did his father-hood unto Adam and his wife, and when he drove them out of the garden he made for them coats of skin, and clothed them.

And Adam begat many children, and his children began to multiply, and desired very eagerly to multiply from time to time exceedingly, that they might take posses-sion of the whole earth. And this great eagerness will be understood concerning the daughters of Lot who thought all men being destroyed from the face of the earth, and thus bare children to their father.

The word of God that is written in the Pentateuch, thus said he : The thought of

man's heart is evil from his youth ; even
this shall not be forgotten.

And so was his first-born son who
was called Cain ; he slew his brother Abel
for jealousy, and also repented for his evil
deed, and took from Adam's daughters one
as his wife, and parting from his father he
went forth into a far off country.

After Cain had parted from his father,
Seth became before Adam his first-born
son. The great sorrow of God ought not
to be forgotten forever, when he thought
to destroy the people of Adam by the
flood of waters, even the work of six eternities, the crown of his creation : it grieved
the Lord in his heart exceedingly, for all
the men who were on the earth, contrary
to God's spirit, filled the earth with evil
and violence. And God was aggrieved in
his heart, for the Lord asked, to his holiness
and his justice, the question whether the
work of six eternities shall be destroyed in
a moment, by forty days' flood of waters
from the face of the earth. Henceforth the
word of God spoken by hand of the

prophet, Isaiah ix, 12, will be so well
understood how he said: I will make man
more worth than fine gold, even the man
more praised than the gold of Ophir.
And the Lord rejoiced when he saw
Noah being a wise man who walked after
the spirit of God, but God counted for the
lost men again one hundred and twenty
years that they shall hearken to the voice
of Noah; and in face of this people he
built his ark. And Noah bought from this
people wives for his three sons, and also
took servants in sufficient number that they
help him to finish his ark. And those men
were bought as slaves, and it may be perhaps that Noah could not buy maid servants for them because of the jealousy of
the chiefs and men of rank. And thence-
forth these servants dwelt with Noah and
his sons together in the ark, when the
flood of waters fell upon the earth. And
the Pentateuch told a short word that at
the time of Noah many men were by their
names known for their strength, for their
cunning; they thought themselves as the

children of God and mighty men, and because of their great lustfulness they polluted themselves with all beasts that may bring forth strange seed, and that they may multiply perception and knowledge concerning the creation of the stranger seed. And thereafter they did not know the meaning of sin. And when God brought forth in the heart of Adam and his wife the knowledge of good and evil it was good before the eyes of the Lord, but their children destroyed the probation of heart entirely, even the spirit of God, and putting this to scorn and laughter, they filled the face of the whole country with their pollution and with their violence.

Henceforth the word of the Lord spoken by the hand of Isaiah v. will be fully understood. So said he:

Let me sing for my wellbeloved a song of my beloved touching his vineyard. My wellbeloved hath a vineyard in a very fat hill, and he digged a trench about it, and gathered the stones out thereof, and planted it with the choicest vines, and

built a tower in the midst of it, and also
hewed out a winepress therein : and he
looked that it should bring forth grapes,
and why brought it forth wild grapes?
And now, O inhabitants of Jerusalem,
and men of Judah, judge, I pray you, be-
twixt me and my wellbeloved. What
should have been done more to my vineyard that I have not done to it? Wherefore
when I looked that it should bring forth
grapes, brought it forth wild grapes? And
now, I will show, tell you what I will do
to my vineyard: I will take away the
hedge thereof, and it shall be to pasturage;
I shall break down the fence thereof, and
it shall be trodden down; and I will lay it
waste ; it shall not be pruned nor hoed,
but there shall come up briers and thorns;
I will also command the clouds that they
rain no rain upon it. For the vineyard of
the Lord of hosts is the house of Israel,
and the men of Judah his plant of delight.
And he looked for judgment, but behold,
shedding of blood was there ; for righteousness, but behold, cry was there.

But Noah built before his people a great ship pursuant to God's word, and took from all animals, and from all living things that were on the face of the earth the male and female, and brought them into the ship. And this strange work became in the mouth of all his people the object of laughter and mockery.

The word of Christ on the flood of waters shall not be forgotten. The flood of waters fell suddenly upon the people of Noah; and all beasts remaining at the time of Adam's birth, and having likeness of man perished in the waters with all men, and all living souls that were on the face of the earth together, and also great beasts terrible with their figures, and from which Noah had not taken any one after God's command died.

When the flood of waters ceased, the sun arose, and behold, on the heaven there was seen a very great bow, very beautiful in colors, and it shone upon the earth many days as long as the sun rose each day till the waters passed away from the face of earth. And Noah and his children and their servants were witnesses of the bow of the Lord. According to the child-like spirit of men the Lord God said unto Noah, and unto his sons with him, so is it:

And I, behold I establish my covenant with you, and with your seed after you, and with every living creature that is with you, the fowl, the cattle, and every beast of the earth with you ; of all that go out of the ark, even every beast of the earth. And I will establish my covenant with you ; neither shall all flesh be cut off any more by the waters of the flood ; neither shall there any more be a flood to destroy the earth. And thence God said :

This is the token of the covenant which I make between me and you, and every living creature that is with you, forever. I do set my bow in the cloud, and it shall be for a token of the covenant between me and the earth. And when I shall cover the heaven with the cloud over the earth my bow shall be seen in the cloud, and I will remember my covenant which is between

me and you and every living creature of all
flesh ; and the waters of the flood shall no
more be there again to destroy all that is
clothed by flesh. And the bow shall be
in the cloud, and I will look upon it that I
may remember the everlasting covenant
between God and every creature that has
living soul, and that is clothed with flesh on
the earth.

And God said unto Noah: This is the
token of the covenant which I have
set up between me and all over the earth
that is clothed by flesh.

The bow of God is in truth the hope of
the Lord, for he foresaw the good that
shall come from the seed of Noah, and
even for this the Lord expected that at the
coming time all men shall understand the
ways of God's spirit, and shall from their
heart choose and love, to walk in the way
of judgment, and righteousness.

And henceforth the waters of the flood
shall not be there a second time, forever,
but when God rises to judge over the earth,
the fire of his wrath shall burn upon the earth.

The covenant of the heart's language is established between the child, and his father, and his mother, between man and man ; and when the man and his wife begat the child, a strong covenant was there between them, and henceforth the covenant of the Lord which is established with all living souls, with man and animals that were created from since six eternities, will be well understood. And the man loving his wife knew her, and she conceived, and bare to him a child with pain and sorrow, and when the man saw how this child was after his image he loved it, and they both guarded the child with pain and sorrow, and when the child knew his parents a strong covenant was there in their hearts between themselves. And when the animals brought forth the young upon the earth, the mother loved her young from all her soul, but when the young grew, it went forth from the side of the mother, and also the mother sent it off at the time of its growing.

And thus God after six eternities full of

pain and sorrow created Adam, the likeness
of the Lord, and gave to man right and
command for life, that it may take root in
his heart, and stay in man's heart. And
it is the full longing of God to rest, to
dwell in man's heart. And it is not upon
the elevated height nor in the handsome
house, be it from fine stone, be it from
costly gold. And this is the Sabbath of
the Lord, that his likeness, the children of
man, shall know the good work of God
their father, by their hearts, and guard it,
and shall praise the wonderful creation of
God by exploring it from all their soul.
Therefore God on the seventh day had
given to man the Sabbath, that man shall
from time to time learn the meaning
of the Sabbath. And the Sabbath of God
shall be kept within the heart of man
from child to his child, for after God had
fought and conquered the darkness and
emptiness in six eternities with a great
deal of pain and sorrow that shall never be
comprehended by man, even in the seventh
eternity, there was Sabbath unto the Lord.

And this is the Sabbath of the Lord that
the everlasting life which he gave unto
man, the likeness of God, had conquered
the darkness, and emptiness. Henceforth
it shall become very much to every man to
keep the Sabbath holy from week to week
after the thought of his heart, after the
advice of wise men. And this is the bow
of the Lord that is seen in the cloud, for
ever, that the living of man, the everlasting life, is established before the face of
the Lord.

Prior to the time of Noah there were
several languages spoken among men ; but
after the flood of waters, Noah, three sons
with him, their wives and their servants
remained on the earth.

Therefore Noah was called the father of
all man's seed. And after Noah the whole
earth was of one language, and of one
speech. And the children of Noah knew
that their multiplication over the earth
shall bring scattering surely and thus they
thought to hinder their scattering by the
building of a tower which shall go up unto

heaven. And the Lord came down to see
the city, and the tower, which the children
of Adam built. And the Lord said, Behold they are one people and they have all
one language, and this is what they begin
to do ; and now shall it not be withholden
from them which they purpose to do. Go
to, let us go down, and there confound
their language that they may not understand one his next's speech. And the
Lord raised among them fiery jealousy, and
in that country was fiery strife, but Nimrod who was called a mighty hunter before
the Lord, conquered his enemy, and built
Babel thereon. Many families of Noah's
generation being conquered withdrew before Nimrod far off that they might seek
good country, and dwell therein, but their
children after much time were changing,
and forgetting the language of Noah. And
thus it will be understood, this is the will
of God, that men shall fill the earth for
dominion, and that their language shall
vary among them, and that for this cause
intellect and knowledge shall multiply

among them pursuant to the spirit of God.

God, before Adam and his wife destroyed their parents, the likenesses of man, from the earth, for the likeness of God had not yet come upon them. And from the sons of Adam he took Noah, and made him again the father of man, by the token of his covenant, for God expected to see for man the coming of good times. And the Lord being a true father and holy God showed before little man, before Noah and his children, the bow of heaven in the cloud, and by short words said unto them : This bow that is seen in the cloud shall be a token of the covenant that is between God and all living souls that are on the earth : but when man learns to understand the meaning of the bow of the Lord, be. hold the sublime thought of God that was hidden from man's reasoning is revealed before the wise men. The bow of the Lord shall show the hope of the Lord for the time that shall come from the cloud out over man. And henceforth from among the children of Noah he chose

Abram, and said unto him: Get thee out
of thy country, and from thy kindred and
from thy father's house, unto the land that
I will show thee, and I will make of thee a
great nation, and I will bless thee and
make thy name great, aud be thou a blessing, and I will bless them that bless you,
and them that curse you will I curse, and
in thee shall be blessed all the generations
of the earth.

When the Lord created heaven and
earth he said to his Godhood: I will give
to man the earth, and all that is in the
earth, even unto my likeness; and after
man had multiplied on the earth I will
give the earth to the man who is of my
likeness, and who walks with me. And
the earth, after my work of six eternities,
shall not be in vain, but at the coming
time shall the earth be filled with man
who is fully of my likeness, and who walks
with me. And, thereafter, the Sabbath of
delight shall be unto me from eternity
until eternity. Henceforth the word of
Moses spoken unto Joshua son of Nun will

be thus well understood; thus it is: Art
thou jealous for my sake? Would God
that all the people were prophets, that the
Lord would put his spirit upon them!

God is the truthful father, and the holy
God, and this the being of the Lord is seen
in the Pentateuch, and in all holy books.
And after God had finished the work of
six eternities, thus said he: Behold, I have
given you every herb yielding seed, which
is upon the face of all the earth, and every
tree yielding seed, and every fruit of the
tree that bears fruit, to you it shall be
for food, and to every beast of the earth
and to every fowl of the air, and to every
thing that creepeth upon the earth, wherein
there is living soul, I have given every green
herb for food. And it was so. And God
saw every thing that he had made, and,
behold it was very good. And there was
evening and there was morning, sixth
eternity. *Eternity.* And what is this
word? Behold, the answer is found
readily. The prayer of Moses, the man of
the Lord in Psalm 90 shall be thus read:

A thousand years in thy sight are but as yesterday which passeth away, and as a watch in the night.

Unto the Lord it is an easy thing that he create all the world by short times. In the holy scriptures there were several stories that the dead became living because of the will of God. But the Lord is sublime in His Godhood; elevated in His spirit, and in all His council there is no vain thing.

Behold, when man with his wife begets his likeness, when they raise up the child by sorrow and guard it, this is the fruit of their labor, of their painful strain unto them, and hence it becomes being honored, being blessed unto them. And the gold of Ophir could not bring away the fruit of man, the child, out from his heart. And when man with his wife raise up the child several years with all their love, and guard, it becomes a glorious work unto them; and it is forbidden within his heart and within his thought, that the child, the fruit of his labor of much time, of his

THE LOST AGES. 41

sorrow, shall be good for nothing. And,
behold, the word of God ought never to be
forgotten, and it is written in the Pentateuch that man was created in the image
of God, in the likeness of God. And
when the child grows up strong, it becomes
thus a Sabbath unto his parents. And,
too, these parents shall bless their Sabbath
within their heart. And, thereafter, the
word of the Lord will be very well understood, how it happened, that He after six
eternities of labor blessed his Sabbath, and
hallowed it, at the time of Adam's birth.

The holiness of God could not be unto
telling, unto writing within the Pentateuch
that God created all the world in six
eternities. At that former time the intellect of man was still hidden before the face
of the Lord. And in the spirit of God
there is no haughty thing, but he had thus
spoken unto man, unto Adam and his
children that he had created heaven and
earth, all the being of the earth in six
days. And by the Lord the sublime
thought was there written, that man from

generation to generation till the face of the earth to his use, and, thereafter, till the words of God to the light of his heart.

And when the children of Israel saw in the wilderness the manna that rained from heaven, they spake the one to another: This white thing, that lies on the face of the wilderness, what is that? And Moses said unto the children of Israel: This is your bread, given by the Lord.

And the Sabbath of the Lord, that he blessed on the seventh day and hallowed it, wherefore is it? And for this question the answer is here that the Lord God had created heaven and earth in six eternities, and the Lord had given the just commandment, the law of truth to man that he remember to hallow the Sabbath of the Lord within his heart.

And Moses, the man of the Lord called by his prayer like in Psalm 90, so said he: The time of our years is seventy years, and even if it holds strong, eighty years, yet their pride is but labor and sorrow, for it is gone flighty, and we go by flying. So teach us, that we bring in our heart toward wisdom, number our days.

Therefore it becomes to every man that he remember to hallow the Sabbath of the Lord each week, for the lifetime of man is short, the time of seventy years. And to every man it is commanded that he till the ground of the Sabbath of the Lord, that he sow the reason of the Sabbath of God in all the spirit of man and that he eat the fruit of this labor to the glory of God their creator.

And when man by one moment begets the child, it shall come well nigh that a great many children should be unto this man; this father would be capable to destroy many children as good for nothing, and his heart should be filled with vain thought and cursing. And, if God created heaven and earth, and, to the very word, the earth alone in six days, this God could be unto destroying of the whole earth many times again; and therefore the Sabbath of the Lord should go in vain, and in man's heart sublime thoughts for praising his God could not take root there.

And when God saw that the wickedness
and violence of the children of Adam prevailed and increased exceedingly on the
face of the earth, he was aggrieved in his
heart for he saw his Sabbath that was
after his labor of six eternities now thus
being defiled and destroyed. And again
he gave for the children of Adam one hundred and twenty years that the seed of the
goodly and righteous shall be found upon
the earth in sufficient number. And when
the Lord found Noah being a righteous
man he was exceedingly delighted with
such delight, whose height man shall never
comprehend. And he saved Noah and his
children thus from the flood of waters, and
established with them an everlasting
covenant, and thereafter, the Sabbath of the
Lord was returning there. And the being
of the earth, and the living of man was
again good in the face of the Lord; hence
God set up in the cloud the token of his
hope, the great bow; and this bow thus
established the Sabbath of the Lord, for
God forsaw that by the coming time of

judgment there shall stay on earth many men being righteous.

And when God brought in man upon the earth he sent things of the tempter in the face of man, for in the council of God there was written that man being in the garden without labor and sorrow, shall not be living forever. Was the playing of the tempter withholden from the face of man the work and creation of the Lord should go like nothing. Hence it is thought by the Lord that a great many men shall fall in their struggle with the tempter and shall fill the house of hell until over its roof, but that few men being like fine gold, like costly stone in the house of God shall find there the everlasting life; this is that God longed for.

And the Lord by his own will let write down throughout the Pentateuch, and the holy books a great many things of the tempter that man from generation to generation shall go free whether he shall understand the word of God or throw it behind. Hence the sayings of wise men,

the teaching of Jesus went into truth; so it
is: Blessed are the poor in spirit, for
theirs is the kingdom of heaven.

And in the Pentateuch there is written
about this very thing, so it is. And the
Lord God created man from the dust of
the earth and breathed in his nostrils the
breath of life, and man became living soul.
And, behold, the poor in spirit believe
readily that word of creation, but to the
men who hold themselves as being wise
men snares are given readily by the Lord
And these men called themselves wise men
therefore they were fools before the Lord
for they talked the story of this creation
to laughter.

By the first man who was called Adam
there was a childish spirit as well as by
his children. Therefore God spake in his
true fatherhood unto Adam and his children the Pentateuch of creation, that
they shoul l keep and deliver the word of
God unto their generation throughout all
times. And unto the Lord it may not be
come to talk for the second time the story

of the creation unto the latter man, for
God had spoken the story of the creation
unto Adam who lived for nine hundred
and thirty years, once one time. See, a
man begat the child, and raised it up, and
thereafter told the story of Lis birth to
his child, and thus the Lord had spoken
unto his son Adam the story of the creation
one time.

This is the first commandment of God
that he gave unto man who was called
Adam : Remember the day of Sabbath
that thou shalt hallow it. Six days shalt
thou labor, and do all thy work. But the
seventh day is the Sabbath of the Lord thy
God, in it shalt thou not do all thy work,
for the Lord had created heaven and earth,
and seas and all that is in them in six days
and rested on the seventh day. Therefore
the Lord blessed the day of Sabbath and
hallowed it.

The birth of man, the day of Adam's begetting was Sabbath unto the Lord. Therefore the just commandment shall come unto every man till forever that he remember

the birth of man, the begetting of Adam on the seventh day each week, and say before his father the Lord praises of delight.

See, ye all of mankind, and hear: remember in your hearts, and keep it; the Lord your father shall have delights of heaven when you understand the Sabbath of the Lord, the day of your birth, and when you make this day the day of hallelu· jah and praises.

The mockers that are in mankind shall do mockery about that narration of the Pentateuch. Thus it is: God created man of the dust of the earth, and breathed through his nostrils the breath of life, and man became a living soul. And also the mockers shall mock about the creation of Adam and his wife, for it was written in the Pentateuch how woman was made from the bone of man.

In this narration of the Pentateuch the snare is there seen that shall catch the man who loves evil and sin. And this man refused to believe in that word of the

Pentateuch, and hence he was saying : In
all the world there is no Lord nor from
the Gods any one, and I shall go ahead to
do sin, and I shall run to think evil
thoughts, for there is no Lord or God who
punishes sin.

This is the will of God that man shall
struggle with the tempter all times, and
at the end shall be there a conqueror
or a conquered. Therefore the Lord had
called every man by the name Israel, for
he had struggled with God and man, and
prevailed against them.

And in the Pentateuch, when it spoke
of the creation of heaven and earth, there
is much riddle by the Lord, that every
man shall strain his soul to lifting up, and
to investigation of that riddle. And man
became honored by his earthly work, but
he became more elevated for the labor of
his spirit, and thereafter was numbered as
a child of the Lord.

The mockery of the mocker shall take
to holding its peace before this narration.
Thus it is :

The spirit of God is the beginning of all. And, thereafter, the spirit of God moved upon the waters. On the face of heaven there is no end. And there were the elements of water scattered, but there on all the face of heaven was darkness, in the high and deep. And, the spirit of God was moving amidst the waters. And thereafter, the waters were awakening up, and the flames of fire came out thereof. And on the face of heaven the fires moved with the waters to and fro, but until the flames of fire multiplied in their scattering there was first eternity. And behold there was light in all face according to the word of God. And when the flame of fire came into a place there was light, and hence was called day, but when this flame went behind the elements of waters, there was again darkness, and this was called night.

In the midst of the first eternity the seed of firmaments being made by the fires were separated from the waters, and thus many firmaments began their existence.

And all this was before the existence of our earth. And hence God called the multitude of these firmaments Heaven, but it was not written in the Pentateuch how God saw for the creation of heaven that it was good, for he is making forever of many new firmaments after the existence of our earth on the face of heaven. And among those firmaments there was the existence of the sun, our sun. And also the seed of our earth began in its place its growing. And all this was in the second eternity.

But our earth was finished in the midst of the third eternity, and the earth began to bring forth all the herb wherein is the seed, and the tree wherein is the seed, and which bears its fruit. And all this became good at the end of the third eternity.

And unto our earth the exact sign of day and year had not yet come until the sun, and the moon, and the stars, with them together, perfected their course in their rising, and going down well, that they separate upon the earth between day and night, and that they give unto our earth perfect signs for day, for year, for time. And all this was in the fourth eternity.

In the midst of the fourth eternity, the seed of the fish wherein is living soul was moving within the water according to the word of God. But within the water the seed of the fish was male, and there was yet no female by it. Many fish and things that moved in the water perished for their lustfulness. And from all these one male fell very sick by its lustfulness, and there-after threw a bone from its body, and thus the female seed began its growing by the side of the male. And that male guarded the female and begat with her the young; and all this was by the side of the water. And from the water the seed of the fowl came. And the inhabitants of the water being male began to move upon the earth, but a great many perished, and few out of them remained that could dwell upon the earth and upon the water. And behind the male the female creeping began to go forth from the water, and begat with the males the offspring upon the earth. And until the offspring multiplied in seed, there were several kinds that returned not to the water. And from these the fowls came forth, and began to fly under the heaven. And God saw it that it was good. And the multitude of the fish and fowls grew up unto their perfection. And God blessed them thus, saying: Be fruitful and multiply, and fill the waters in the seas, and let fowl multiply on the earth.

And the creeping things that went forth from the water perished upon the earth, for breath was not going through their nostrils. And few caught breath according to the spirit of God and became living upon the earth, but the breath was not yet strong unto them, and they returned to the water, but came again upon the earth until the breath was strengthened in the nostrils. And all this was in the fifth eternity.

Several kinds that went forth from the

fish got wings that they fly above the water. And from these the seed of the fowl went forth, but they were bound to the water much time, until another kind was there, that flew under heaven and returned no more to the water. From the small seed of the creeping things in the water went forth great sea monsters after much time, and also from the small fowl came forth the eagle after much time. From the creeping in whose nostrils the breath was strengthened went forth all beasts of the field after their kind, and the animals of the earth after their kind. The creation of these animals began in the midst of the fifth eternity, and was finished until the midst of the sixth eternity by their kinds, according to the spirit of God. And God saw it that it was good.

And God said: Let us make man in our image, after our likeness; and let them have dominion over the fish of the sea, and over the fowl of the air, and over the cattle, and over all the earth, and over every creeping thing that creepeth upon the

And God created man in his own image, in the image of God created he him ; male and female created he them.

In the midst of the sixth eternity, from the monkey the seed of man went forth, but was perfected until the end of the sixth eternity, being male and female, according to the spirit of God. And many peoples having likeness of man perished out from the face of the earth, for the likeness of God had not yet come upon them. And when from these men Adam and his wife came up in the garden, God blessed them, and God said unto them : Be fruitful, and multiply, and replenish the earth, and subdue it, and have dominion over the fish of the sea, and over the fowl of the air, and over every living thing that moveth upon the earth. And God said : Behold, I have given you every herb yielding seed, which is upon the face of all the earth, and every tree and the fruit of the tree bringing forth fruit, and yielding seed, to you it shall be for food, and to every beast of the earth and to every fowl of the air, and to every creeping thing that creepeth upon the earth wherein is living soul, I have given every green herb for food, and it was so.

And God saw everything that he had made, and, behold, it was very good. And there was evening, and there was morning, sixth eternity.

And throughout the Pentateuch it was there written, six times, there was evening and there was morning, for each day; and wherefore is it so?

The answer is it that before the face of God, in the language of the Lord, one eternity is like a day of man, for in the language of man one eternity is there not known.

And when man, the likeness of God, was not yet there upon the earth, unto the Lord there was no Sabbath. And when God saw man having not the likeness of God he destroyed man after his right, for God had not yet found his Sabbath. But when man having likeness of God was found on the earth there was Sabbath unto

:he Lord. Therefore God blessed this day
ind hallowed it. Within the thought of
nan eternity and the meaning of eternity
vas not known. Therefore God gave the
verlasting commandment unto man that
every man remember to hallow his Sabbath on the seventh day. And the Lord
is supreme in his holiness, and the heart
of the Lord is full of holy and truthful
thought. And thus the Lord appeared
unto Moses and said unto him, thus it is: I
will make all my goodness pass before
thee, and will proclaim the name of the
Lord before thee; and I will be gracious
to whom I am gracious, and will show
mercy on whom I have mercy. Thou
canst not see my face, for man shall not
see me and live. And the Lord said:
Behold, there is a place by me, and thou
shalt stand upon the rock, and when my
glory passeth by I will put thee in a cleft
of the rock, and will cover thee with my
hand, until I have passed by, and I will
take away mine hand, and thou shalt see
my back, but my face shall not be seen.

And hence God spoke unto man: My
back shalt thou see, but my face shall not
be seen.   And what are these words?
And it is the answer that the spirit of
God is the beginning of all, and from
since eternity until eternity he labored
and created until man was created at the
latter time.   Therefore God said unto
man: My back shalt thou see, but my
face shall not be seen.

The full longing of God is for that he
make his Sabbath in the heart of every
man.   The Sabbath of the Lord was not
above in heaven, but, after he had created
man upon the earth, he wanted to rest in
the heart of every man. Thus the Sabbath
of the Lord shall be in man's heart forever.

And Moses said unto the children of
Israel, thus it is: For this day when I
bide thee commandment is not hidden nor
far off from thee.   Nor is it in heaven,
when thou sayest, who could go up for us
toward heaven and bring it down to us
that we may hear and do it?   And nor is
it beyond the sea, and when thou sayest,

who could pass over the sea for us and bring up it to us that we may hear and do it? Only but the word is very near unto thee, that thou put it in thy mouth and in thy heart. The word of the Lord came unto Solomon, thus said he:

This is the house which thou art building, if thou wilt walk in my statutes and execute my judgments, and keep all my commandments to walk in them, then will I establish my word with thee, which I spake unto David, thy father. And I will dwell among the children of Israel, and will not forsake my people, Israel. Hence it becomes to every man that he build his sanctuary within his heart, for the spirit of God is hating all wickedness. And the spirit of God is filled with holiness and truth, and is loving all goodness and all judgment.

And the everlasting Sabbath of the Lord is in the heart of the righteous man, and the delightful resting of God is in the thought of the goodly man. And this is the holy secret of the Lord.

End of the First Volume.

ATTENTION.

The name of the author will be given out in due time, when all benefits of international rights shall be assured for him. A brief sketch of the translator's life is here given : A native of Hungary, he was educated in the Vienna Deaf Mutes Institution, and was also a former pupil of Mr. Greenberger, Principal of the Improved Institution for the Deaf, Lexington Avenue, New York. Since 1875 he became an inhabitant and citizen of the United States under the name "Francis Rother," while his family name was Franz Rotter. Being eager from his youth to become one of the pioneers of the coming Ethiopian civilization, he studied the Abyssinian languages and received an invitation by King John of Abyssinia to enter his empire. But he was hindered from being welcomed by his Ethiopian majesty by the war condition that prevailed there (1887–1888.) He was called and known by the mute society and their newspaper under the by-word " Round World." As the other seven volumes, being written in Ethiopian, require much labor and are likely to be followed by others, and ought to be spread in many languages, the aid of an enterprising publisher is wanted.

Apply to address of translator as found in face cover of the book.

www.ingramcontent.com/pod-product-compliance
Lightning Source LLC
Chambersburg PA
CBHW020731100426
42735CB00038B/1881